Energy And Action

MOTION AND SPEED

John Marshall, Ed.D.

The Rourke Book Co., Inc.
Vero Beach, Florida 32964

PHOTO CREDITS
All photos © J.M. Patten

Library of Congress Cataloging-in-Publication Data

Marshall, John, 1944-
    Motion and speed / John Marshall.
        p. cm. — (Energy and action)
    Includes index.
    Summary: Briefly describes the concepts, measurement, and laws
of motion.
    ISBN 1-55916-154-X
    1. Motion—Study and teaching—Juvenile literature. 2. Speed—
Study and teaching—Juvenile literature. [1. Motion.] I. Title. II. Series
QC133.5.M37 1995
531'.112—dc20   95-17283
                                            CIP
                                            AC

Printed in the USA

TABLE OF CONTENTS

WHAT IS SCIENCE?

Science is a way of finding out how things happen. Do you run, throw a ball or ride a bicycle around the block? In science, running, throwing and pedaling are all kinds of **motion** (MOH shun).

Did you know that you are in motion, or moving, every second, all day and all night? Wait! How can this happen?

Let's read all about motion and speed, and find out why you're moving even when you're sleeping.

The push of the rider's feet on the pedals makes his bike move.

MOTION IS MOVEMENT

Scientists say that anything moving is "in motion." Objects that look like they're not moving are said to be "at rest."

Think about a ride on a school bus. As you ride, trees, houses and parked cars look like they are going by. You know the bus is moving down the road.

These kids are "in motion," getting on the bus to ride home from school.

When you ride on your seat inside a bus, are you moving or not moving?

People out on the sidewalks watch the bus go by and see you in motion. However, inside the bus, are you and the friend sitting next to you moving?

Are you moving or not moving?

The answer is you're moving *and* not moving. You are "at rest" in your seat, but you are also "in motion" down the road on the bus.

EVERYTHING IS ALWAYS IN MOTION

Everything, including you, rocks, trees and houses are in motion every moment of every day. Everything is moving with the Earth as it rotates each day and revolves in its yearly orbit around the sun.

The Earth is always moving steadily along. That's why night becomes day, the seasons change and time passes.

We don't feel this movement because everything on Earth moves together, just as you and your friend felt "at rest" on the moving school bus.

Even when you hold still for a picture, you're moving because the Earth is moving.

SPEED TELLS HOW FAST

Some things move along slowly, like jammed-up traffic and old tortoises. Others, like trains and subway cars, move so fast they're a big blur as they pass by.

Speed (SPEED) is how fast an object is moving. It is measured by how much time something takes to get from one place to another.

The winner of a 100-meter race moves from the starting line to the finish line faster, or at a greater speed, than all the other runners.

This moving car is a blur as it goes by.

SPEED AND DISTANCE

Speed tells how fast an object is going. Knowing your speed is important. Speeding out of control, like running headlong down steep stairs or drag racing in a car, is very dangerous.

Distance tells how far an object has traveled. Airplane pilots and other drivers must keep track of how far they've gone to be sure of where they are.

Airplane pilots must know how far they've gone to be sure where they are.

Neighborhood speed limits are slow for safety.

A **speedometer** (speh DAHM eht er) measures how fast cars and trucks are moving. An **odometer** (oh DAH meht er) records how far a vehicle has traveled. A pedometer tells how far a person has walked or jogged.

Speed is usually measured in miles-per-hour, or mph. Fifty mph is faster than 30 mph. Road signs tell the safe speed for traveling vehicles.

SPEED + DIRECTION = VELOCITY

Knowing the speed of an object is only half of the story of motion. It is also important to know the direction an object is going. Compass points—like north, south, east and west—tell the direction.

Velocity (veh LAH si tee) is the speed and direction of any moving object.

Without velocity, airplanes would land in very strange places. Pilots wouldn't know how fast to go and what direction to fly!

This windsock at a small airport helps pilots know the wind's direction and speed.

FORCE STARTS MOTION

People have studied motion for thousands of years. In experiments, ancient Greek scientists observed, or noticed, that no object could move by itself. They figured out that a **force** (FORS), like a push or a pull, is needed to start an object moving.

Muscle power is the force that gets people and animals walking, running or jumping. Other energy sources that provide power to move objects include gasoline for cars, electricity for carnival rides and wind for sailboats.

Hands and muscles are the forces that push this basketball toward the hoop.

SIR ISAAC NEWTON

About 300 years ago, a scientist named Sir Isaac Newton learned that the ancient Greeks' idea of motion was only partly right.

Newton, like the Greeks, knew that force was needed to put an object in motion. However, he discovered that if there were no **friction** (FRIK shun), or rubbing force, the object would stay in motion forever.

Friction, caused by sliding, stops this player at the base.

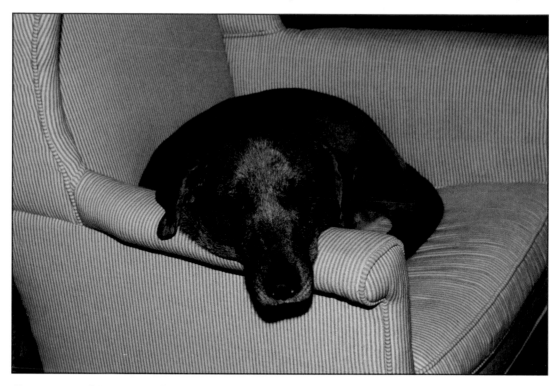

Because of inertia, this dog will stay "at rest" until a force puts her "in motion."

For example, a rolling ball comes to a stop because it rubs against the ground. This friction ends its motion.

This discovery of **inertia** (in ER shuh) was so important it was called *Newton's first law of motion.* Inertia means that an object will stay "at rest" until a force puts it "in motion." Then the object will stay "in motion" until something causes it to stop.

LAWS IN SCIENCE

In science, a **law** (LAW) is a theory, or idea, that has been tested many times with the same results. Scientists test theories over and over to make certain they are correct. Then they become "laws" of science.

Newton made many discoveries about motion that became laws of science. Astronauts traveling to the moon radioed this message back to Earth, "We would like to thank the person who made this trip possible—Sir Isaac Newton."

Isn't science amazing? Newton's 300-year-old discoveries helped us land on the moon!

Energy from gasoline is the force that keeps this fishing boat moving.

GLOSSARY

force (FORS) — the push and pull that makes things move

friction (FRIK shun) — the force created by two objects rubbing together

inertia (in ER shuh) — a law of science that says an object will stay "at rest" until put "in motion," and will stay "in motion" until stopped

law (LAW) — a theory, or idea, in science that has been tested many times with the same results

motion (MOH shun) — movement; an object not "at rest" is "in motion"

odometer (oh DAH meht er) — a machine that records miles traveled

speed (SPEED) — how fast an object is moving

speedometer (speh DAHM eht er) — a machine that measures the speed of cars, trucks and boats

velocity (veh LAH si tee) — the speed and direction of a moving object

This amusement park ride is fun. Its motion is around and around in a circle.

INDEX